STEP-BY-STEP

MAKING COLLAGE

JIM ROBINS AND PHILIP STEELE
ILLUSTRATED BY JIM ROBINS

KING*f*ISHER

KINGFISHER
Kingfisher Publications Plc
New Penderel House
283–288 High Holborn
London WC1V 7HZ
www.kingfisherpub.com

First published in 1993 by
Kingfisher Publications Plc
This edition 2001
10 9 8 7 6 5 4 3 2 1

1TR/1100/SC/HBM(FR)/128JAMA

A CIP catalogue record for this
book is available from the British
Library.

ISBN 0 7534 0578 4

Edited by Deri Robins
Designed by Ben White
Illustrations by Jim Robins
Collages by Jim Robins pp 6-15,
  18-21, 24, 28-39; Deri Robins
  pp 22, 40; Philip Steele pp 17, 40.
Photographed by Rolf Cornell,
  SCL Photographic Services
Cover design by Terry Woodley
Printed in Hong Kong/China

CONTENTS

Collages are pictures made by pasting down scraps of paper and other odds and ends. You will need a pair of scissors, glue, paper and card, and all the bits of junk you can lay your hands on.

Paper and Card

Paper and card are ideal for making collages. Try to build up a collection that includes some of the following: newspaper, magazines, tissue and crêpe paper, wallpaper, sugar paper, wrapping paper, sweet wrappers, kitchen foil, sandpaper, junk mail, envelopes, postcards, tracing paper, smooth and corrugated packing card.

Add texture to paper by scrunching or folding it, or try wrapping it around a pencil to make curls. Or add patterns, by laying the paper over a raised surface and rubbing with a spoon.

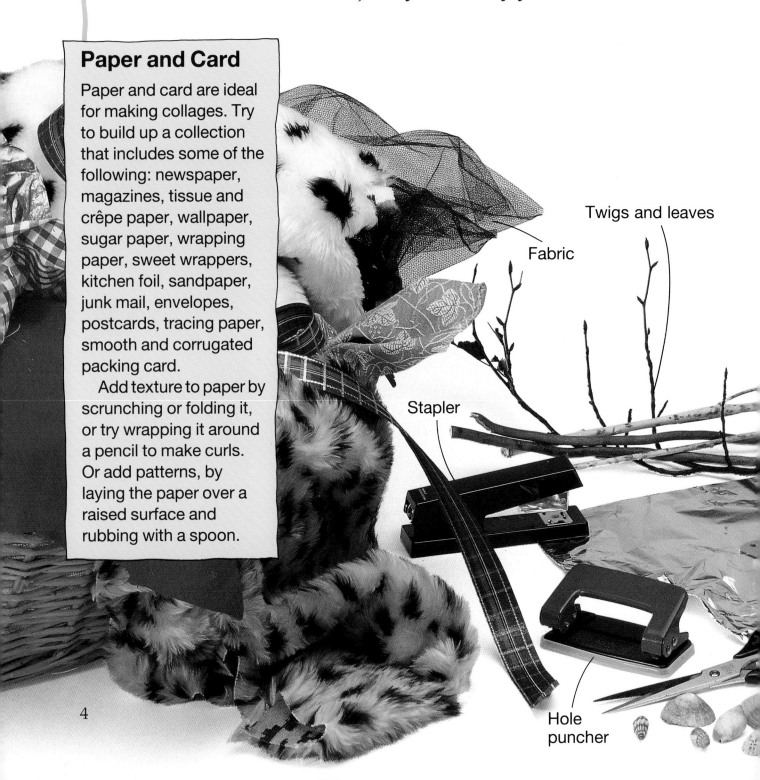

Fabric

Twigs and leaves

Stapler

Hole puncher

4

Fabric

Collages made from fabric are fascinating to touch as well as to look at. Collect scraps of cotton, wool, silk, leather, hessian, lace and netting, as well as ribbons and sequins. Fur fabric is especially fun to work with, and can be bought quite cheaply in small quantities.

Bits and Pieces

Start a junk box, and save the following: egg boxes, string, straws, stamps, buttons, corks, beads, small toys, bits of polystyrene, bubble wrap, screws, washers, nails, nuts and bolts, bottle tops, leaves, shells, twigs and dried pasta.

Tools of the Trade

As well as scissors, you may need to use a craft knife – these are sharp, so ask an adult to help.

Use safe, simple glues, such as PVA, children's gum or glue sticks. Sticky tape and a stapler are also useful.

Although collage is about sticking, you can add extra colour with paints and glitter.

Finally, you will also need a ruler and pencils.

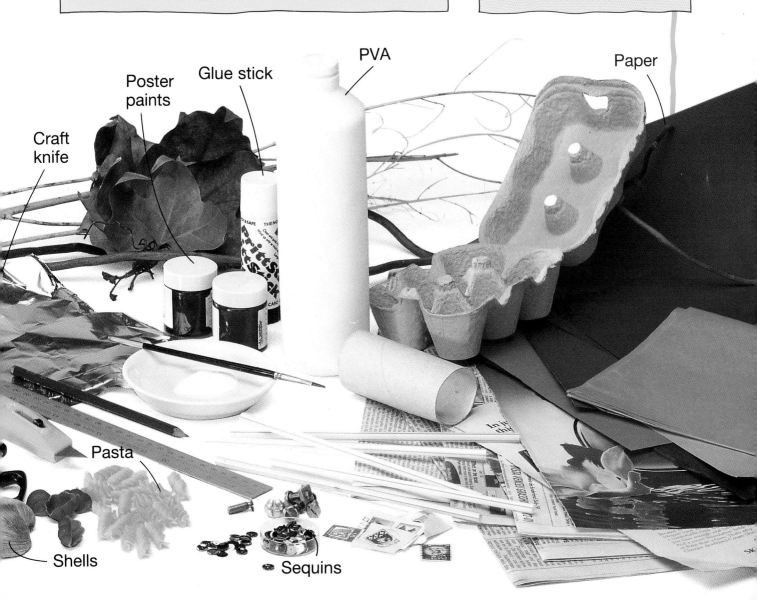

Craft knife

Poster paints

Glue stick

PVA

Paper

Pasta

Shells

Sequins

PAPER PATTERNS

Paper is cheap, colourful and very easy to cut and paste – which makes it perfect for collage. Save old magazines and newspapers, and look out for other types of paper and card (see page 4).

Before you start to make pictures from paper, try arranging scraps in abstract patterns as shown here. Making patterns will help you to learn about colour, shade and texture – this will be helpful not only when making collages from paper, but also when you are using fabric and other bits and pieces.

Try combining cut and torn shapes in your pattern using black and white for bold contrast.

Cut dark-coloured paper into shapes with scissors or a craft knife. Glue them in a pattern onto a sheet of white paper.

In contrast to the clean, sharp lines of the cut paper, a similar pattern made from torn paper has a much softer feel.

For a more subtle contrast, try using the many different *tones* (or shades) of grey that lie between black and white.

Experiment with colour. Try soft pastel shades (below), or bright, cheerful colours. Which ones clash? Which ones work well together?

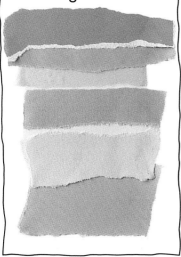

Red, orange and yellow are warm colours. They can appear even warmer when a cool colour is placed next to them, as here.

Blue, green and purple are cool colours. While warm colours appear to come towards you, cool colours often seem to move away.

Try overlapping pieces of tissue paper to make new colours, or to make the same colour deeper.

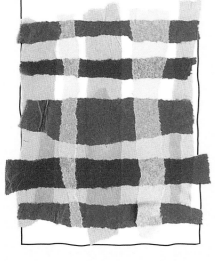

Look for patterns in magazines, wallpaper and wrapping paper. Cut them out, and use them in collage.

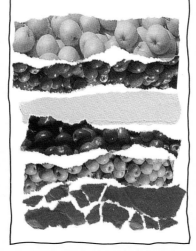

Add texture to your collages, mixing some of the many different types of paper. Add scraps of material, and other finds.

CUT PAPER

Choose strong, bold-coloured paper, and cut it into simple shapes to make striking collages. The one shown here is based on collages by the French artist Henri Matisse – try looking through art books in the library for more ideas.

1 Sketch out your ideas for a collage, using some coloured pencils or crayons.

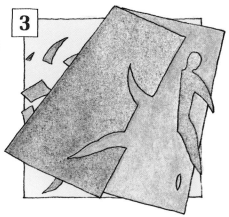

2 Collect paper for the collage. Check that the colours you choose go well together.

3 Cut the paper into shapes, that match those in your drawing. Do the background first.

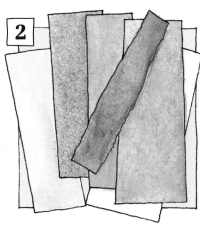

4 Cut out all the other shapes. Arrange the shapes on top of the background.

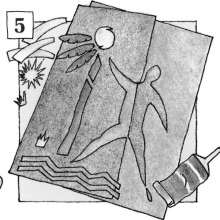

5 Move the shapes around until you like the way they look together. Glue them in place.

TORN PAPER

Pictures made from torn paper have a softer look than those made from cut paper. Tearing produces shapes with a feathery edge – if the paper is coloured on one side and white on the back, you will also get a white line around part of the shape.

1 Sketch out an outline for your collage, and collect your pieces of paper together.

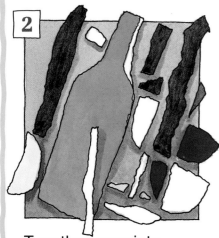

2 Tear the paper into shapes and glue them in place. Overlap with smaller pieces, to add details and highlights.

Make a Mosaic

In Ancient Rome, buildings were often decorated with mosaics – pictures made from tiny pieces of glass or stone set into plaster. Try making a mosaic from tiny squares of torn paper, as here.

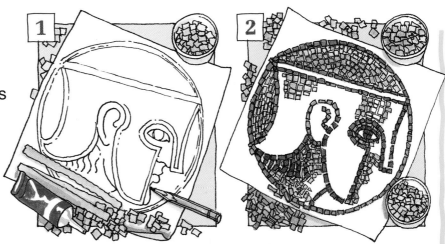

Old magazines are ideal for collage. The paper is glossy, brightly coloured, and full of patterns and letters which add interest to your finished picture. The magnificent crowing cockerel shown below was made from a mixture of torn and cut paper.

1

Make some sketches for your collage on scrap paper, using coloured pencils. Copy the outline onto a piece of card, and use this as a base for the collage.

2

Collect a pile of glossy magazines. Look for large areas of colour, and tear these out. It doesn't matter if the pages have writing or pictures on them.

3

Tear or cut the pages into shapes for the collage. To make the cockerel's tail feathers, press a round lid onto the paper and tear around the curve.

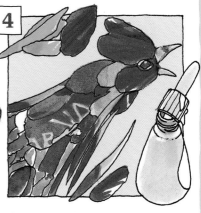

4

Arrange the pieces on top of the card. Try to contrast bright, rich colours with darker areas. Overlap the pieces of paper as shown, and glue down.

WORDS AND PICTURES

Most newspapers are printed in black type on white paper. However, because the size and thickness of the type varies enormously, some areas look very dark while others are light. Try using this variety of *tone* to make pictures.

1

Find a picture with a lot of contrasting tones (in other words, one which contains light, dark and medium shades). Draw the outlines onto card.

2

Look through some newspapers, and tear out pages that have plenty of contrasting light, medium and dark areas of print.

3

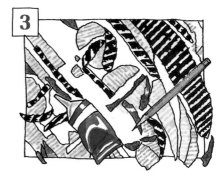

Cut or tear the paper into shapes that match the light and dark areas in your picture. Arrange them in position, and glue them down.

4

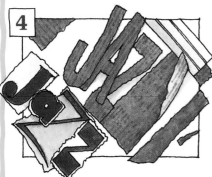

You can finish your picture by adding words – try making these by tearing or cutting letters from the paper.

You can also make words by cutting or tearing out actual letters from headlines in the paper, or from other areas of large type.

Combine the letters with pictures cut from newspapers, photo-copies and magazines – or with drawings you have made yourself.

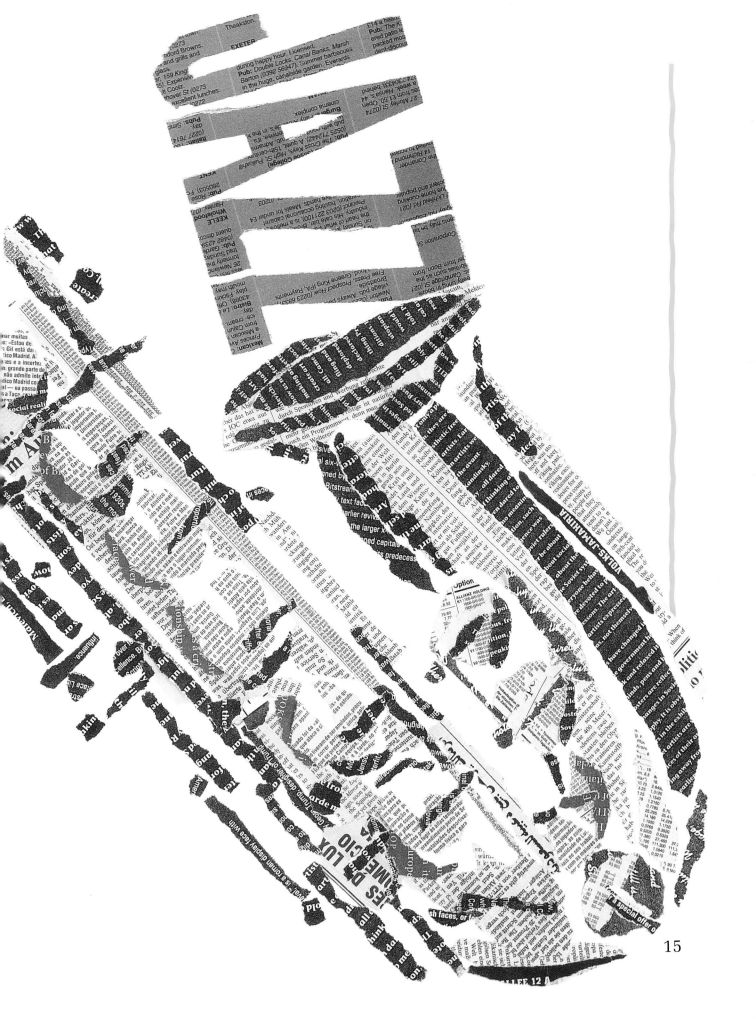

15

STICK-ONS

Some of the best material for collage is thrown away every day. Save used stamps, stickers, labels from tinned food and bottles, seed packets, sweet and biscuit wrappers, sachets of salt and sugar; and glue them down to make pictures.

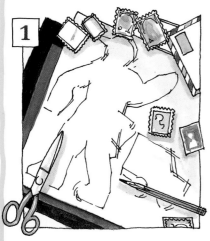

1 Draw a mail van and its driver onto white card. Draw a slightly smaller van and driver on black card, and stick on top.

2 Glue the van and driver onto coloured card or paper. Glue used stamps to the picture, as shown opposite.

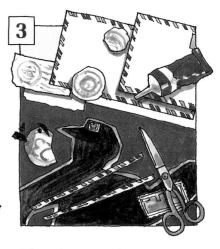

3 Use the envelopes as well – postmarks make good wheels and faces. Add features cut from plain black card.

Cut the labels from tins of fruit, or pictures from colour magazines. Use them to make a collage of a bowl of fruit.

Save sweet wrappers, and glue them onto card to make a picture of a giant toffee!

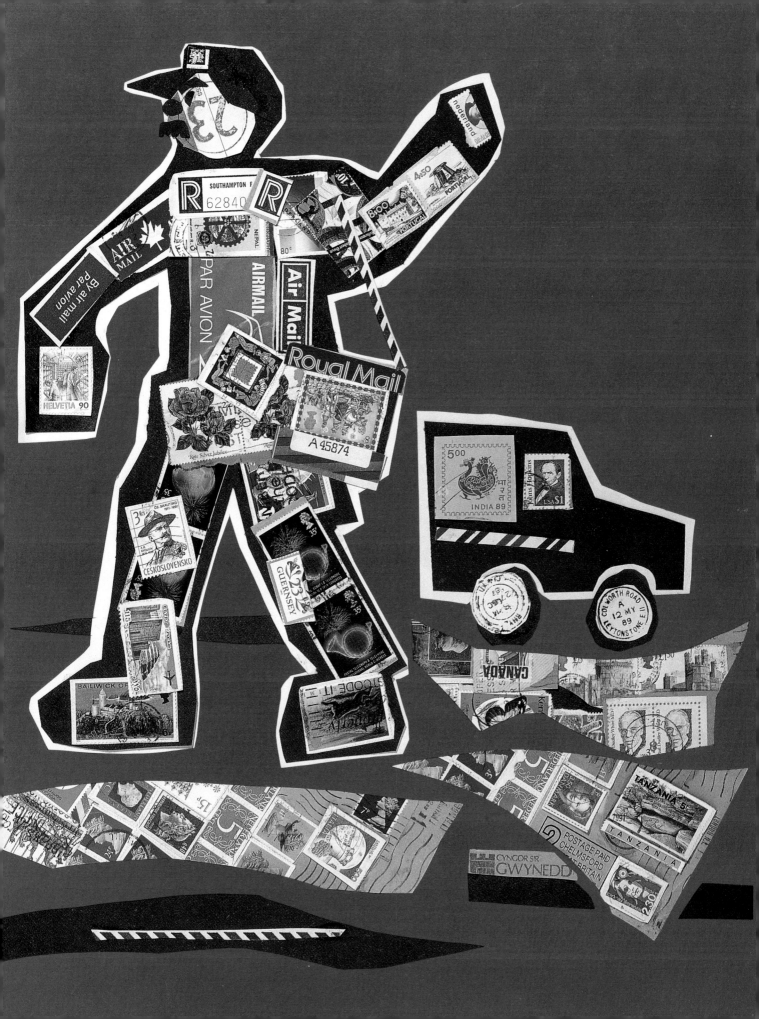

SILHOUETTES

Simple black shapes look dramatic against a light background, or hung up against a window. Draw your design onto thin black card or sugar paper, and cut out the background with scissors or a craft knife. For a stained-glass effect, glue coloured tissue paper to the back of the card.

1

2

3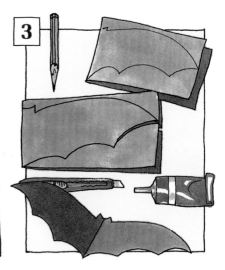

Draw the window frame, witch and castle onto a large sheet of black sugar paper. Cut out the background.

Tape wide strips of tissue paper to the back of the frame. Cut out a moon for the light to shine through.

Fold different-sized strips of black paper in half to make bats. Cut them out, and glue to the window.

Try some more designs – how about a prowling panther in a cage? Stained-glass silhouettes are also popular at Christmas – they often show church windows, but you could try making a snowman, a robin or a Father Christmas.

FUN FABRIC

Fabric collages aren't just interesting to look at – they can be fascinating to touch, too. Collect scraps of material, and see what they suggest to you – velvet is soft and luxurious, plastic is smooth, silk is shiny, hessian is rough and coarse. Add more texture with wool, ribbon, lace and netting.

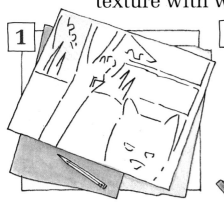

1 Sketch out a design for your collage, and collect your material. To make this jungle scene, we used fur fabric, leather, curtain samples, scrap paper and a plastic bag.

2 Always start with the background. To make a sunset sky, tear orange paper into strips and paste over blue paper.

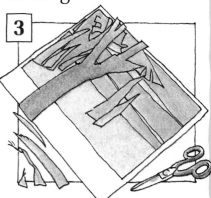

3 Cut and paste down the jungle. The trees at the front are broader than those at the back, to make them look nearer.

4 The leopard is made from fur fabric, while the frog is made from a green plastic carrier bag! Use more scraps to make the features – sequins are good for highlighting the eyes.

FOOD SHAPES

Dried pasta, beans, lentils, tea leaves and eggshells – many types of dried food can be used in collage. This frog is stuck together with glue in the usual way – but you can also make collages that are good enough to eat! Try making a savoury 'collage' on crackers using chopped ham, cheese, and tomato – or press sweets into icing on a cake!

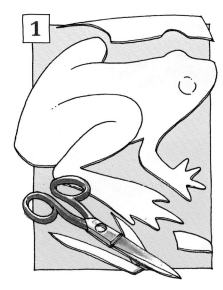

1

Draw a frog onto card, and cut it out. Collect some dried beans, split peas, lentils and large tea leaves.

2

Use a pencil to divide the frog's body into different areas of colour. Cover some of these areas with glue.

3

Take a handful of beans or lentils, and press some of them onto the areas you have covered in glue.

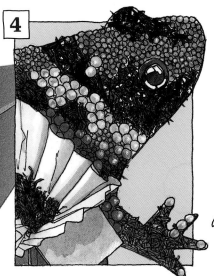

4

Contrast the bright orange lentils with the green peas. Use the tea leaves to make the black stripes on the frog's body. For an eye, you could glue on a circle of black paper.

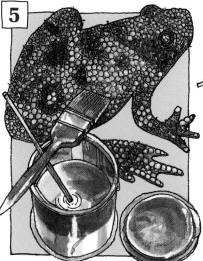

5

Use kitchen foil to add a glimmer to the eye. You can highlight the frog's 'scales' with a little silver paint. Finally, for a shiny wet-look frog, add a coat of polyurethane varnish.

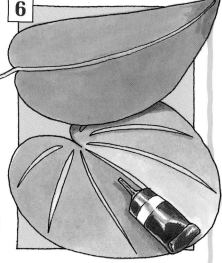

6

Give your frog a leaf to sit on. This can simply be cut from green card or stiff paper, or be made from scraps of fabric material.

SEASCAPE

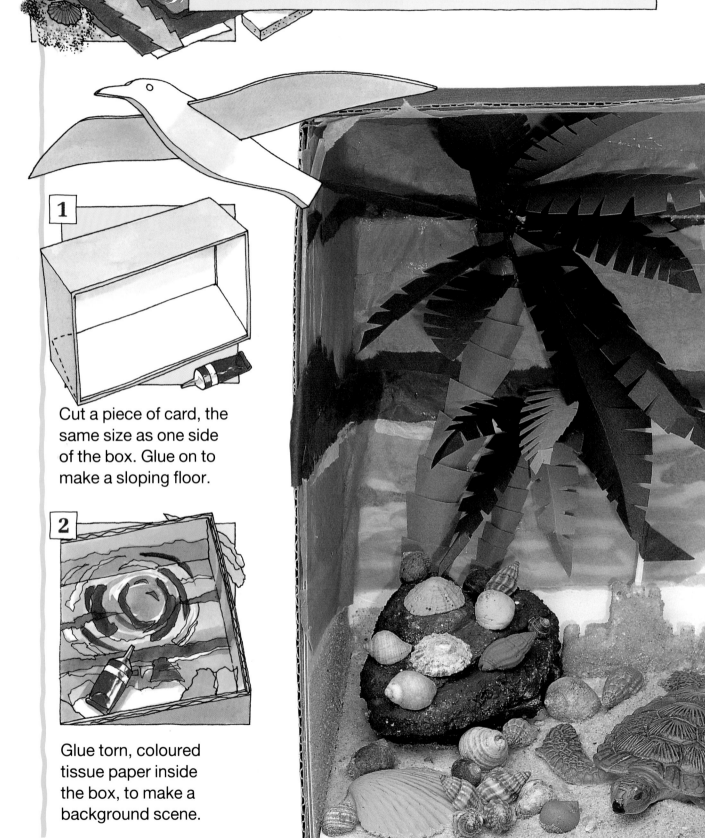

1

Cut a piece of card, the same size as one side of the box. Glue on to make a sloping floor.

2

Glue torn, coloured tissue paper inside the box, to make a background scene.

Don't leave seaside souvenirs to moulder on the windowsill – turn them into a 3-D collage! As well as shells, pebbles and sand, you'll need a cardboard box, tissue paper and thin card. Old toys with a seaside theme can complete the scene.

3

Cut a sandcastle from polystyrene or thick card. Cut circles, and glue into rock shapes.

4

Glue the rocks and castle to the floor. Paint the rocks. Glue shells to the scene.

25

5 Brush the floor and castle with glue and sprinkle on sand. Cut out some tree trunks and leaves from paper.

6 Cut the trunks into segments. Glue each one separately to the back of the box, and tuck in the leaves.

7 Draw gulls' bodies and wings onto white card. Cut a slot in the middle of the bodies for the wings, and hang the gulls from the top of the box with thread. Finally, see if you can find some old toys or decorations to add to your scene.

Left: 3-D collages are a great way of displaying your favourite models!

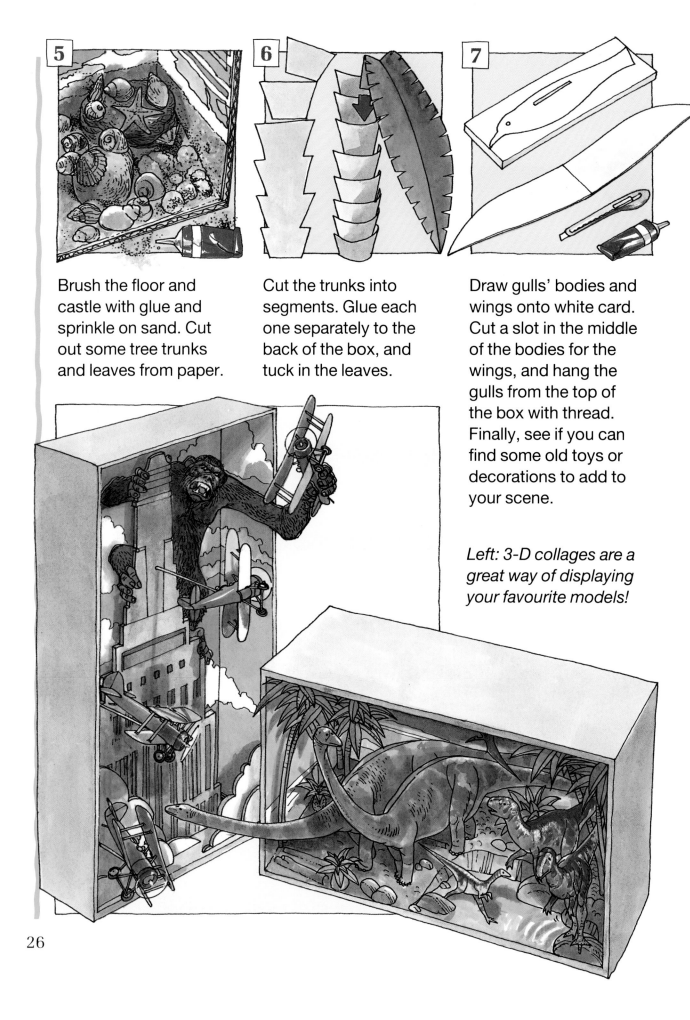

WALL FLOWERS

Once flowers, ferns and leaves have been thoroughly dried or pressed, they should keep forever. Use them simply to make pictures or cards – or combine them with fake flowers to make a window box bursting with colour, like the one overleaf. Never pick wild flowers – they could be very rare.

1

2

3

Pressed Flowers

Press petals, leaves or ferns in a flower press, or between the pages of a heavy book. Leave them to dry for about a month. The flowers can then be glued into a picture with PVA.

Tissue Flowers

1. Make a simple template from card. Use it to cut about ten flowers from tissue paper – use more than one colour, if you like.

2. Staple the flowers together in the centre.

3. Fold up each petal in turn, as shown.

Window Box

This midsummer window box can be made to bloom even in the depths of winter – all you need is some colourful paper and card. If you like, you can also include pressed flowers and leaves, or silk roses like the ones shown in the picture.

1

Cut a window frame from card or paper. Cut a second frame, with slightly thinner bars, and glue this over the first one.

2 Cut a window box from brown paper. Cut out some 'S' shapes, and glue the tips to the window box as shown.

3 Glue all your fake or real flowers to the window box. Fill in the gaps in between with extra leaves cut from coloured card.

29

JUNK MIRROR

Everything from screws and bolts to straws and string can be used in this project. You can also add toys, or figures made from plasticene.

1

Collect together some junk, glue, a small mirror and corrugated card.

2

Cut two bases, each the same size. Cut a hole from one base for the mirror, and glue the two bases together.

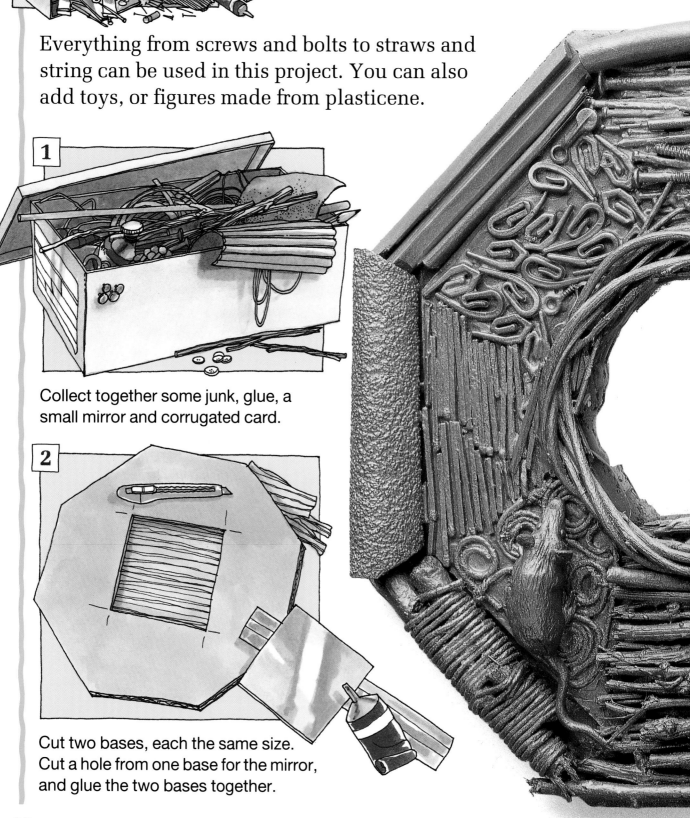

3

Glue the mirror to the centre of the card. Divide the frame into sections, and glue different types of junk to each section. Twist some thin garden twigs to make the circle in the centre.

4

Paint the mirror frame, and seal with a coat of varnish. Ask an adult to help you to attach a picture hook to the back, to hang the mirror up.

31

CRASH!

If an alien intergalactic space cruiser from the year 3000 was to crash unexpectedly through your bedroom wall, it could well look something like this...

1
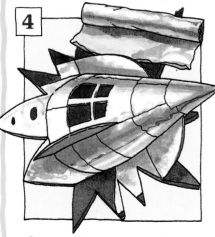

Make a large cone from thin card. Trim the bottom of the cone to make the shape shown.

2

Cut thick card into a starburst shape. Paint it black, and glue or tape on the cone when dry.

3

Cut window holes in the cone. Cut the fins from card, and glue to the top of the cone.

4
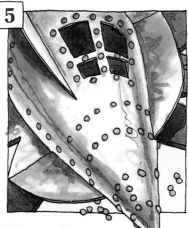

Cover the cone and part of the star with foil, so that it looks like a space ship crashing through a hole.

5

Glue split peas or lentils to the space ship, to look like rivets. Brush the rivets with silver paint.

6

The furious little star ship commander was made from pipe cleaners, beads and coloured paper!

EGGOSAURUS

The last dinosaurs died out about 65 million years ago. Some had razor-sharp teeth. Others had weird-looking crests or knobbly horns. But only the terrifying *Eggosaurus* was made from packing material, egg cartons and plastic bubblewrap...

1 Draw an outline for the *Eggosaurus* onto card, and cut it out. Use it as a template to cut the same shape from bubblewrap, and glue this to the card.

2 Cut up an egg carton, and glue the cups to the body. You can add extra scaly texture with dried peas or beans, seeds, bottle tops, shells or netting.

3 Colour the *Eggosaurus* with thick poster paints. Cut some red ribbon or paper into a tongue, and glue to the mouth.

Stand the Eggosaurus *among trees with plasticene trunks and leaves made from green paper.*

MEMORY BOARD

Holidays, birthdays or a special day out can all be recorded forever in a collage. All you need to do is to save any scraps or souvenirs and glue them onto a board made from card, cork or polystyrene. Hang the board on your wall – every time you look at it, the happy memories will start flooding back!

1

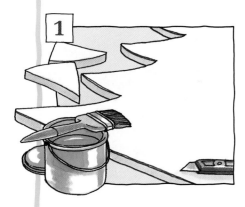

For a Christmas souvenir, cut a piece of thick card into a Christmas tree shape. Paint one side green.

2

Arrange the souvenirs on the board. When you like the way they look together, glue, pin or staple them in place.

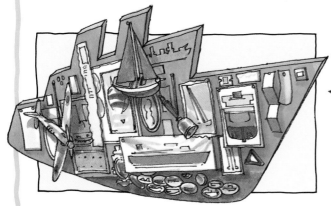

From a dream holiday to a walk in the park, you can use your souvenirs to make a 3-D noticeboard...

COLLAGE CARDS

Home-made cards are a million times nicer than anything you can buy in a shop – ask any mum or dad! A selection of collage ideas from the previous pages of this book was used to make the cards shown below. As well as looking wonderful, they're all incredibly quick and easy to do.

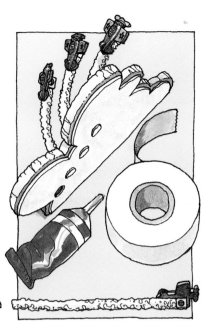

Cut or tear paper into strips, and paste down to make a simple landscape. Use fur fabric or cotton wool to make the sheep in the foreground.

A hole-puncher can be a very useful tool in collage. How else could you make a hundred snowflakes in under a minute?

Four aeroplane-shaped buttons, white pipe cleaners and a cloud cut from a polystyrene tile were used to make this card.

MORE IDEAS

By now you have probably realized that anything that stays still long enough can be turned into a collage. Here are a few ideas you may not have thought of...

Make strange-looking people or animals by cutting up different photos, postcards or pictures and gluing them together. This is called photomontage...

Stick pictures onto lampshades, waste-paper bins, boxes, etc. Or glue dried pasta, sweets or biscuits to the tops of jars. Finish with a coat of varnish...

Collect everything you can on a friend's favourite subject (a sport, film star, hobby etc) and make a collage as a special present.